Mrs. Doreen Saunders,

with best wishes,

+ Bill Down

The
BISHOP'S
BILL of FARE
A Gracious Companion

by

Bishop Bill Down

illustrated by

MarshaRae Ratcliff

BARON
MMV

PUBLISHED in 2005 BY BARON BOOKS of BUCKINGHAM
in association with the Worshipful Company of Carmen
AND PRODUCED BY THE BATH PRESS
with origination by Academic & Technical Typesetting

ISBN 0 86023 680 3

CONTENTS

DEDICATION

For the many friends, in the City of London and in other parts of the world, with whom I have enjoyed good food, good wine and good fellowship, on formal and informal occasions, and recognised that these blessings were a gift from God

Bishop Bill is a priest and also a friend
Whose book 'Bill of Fare' I do recommend.
His deep Christian faith and love of all verse
Produces a menu both rich and diverse.
The Fare in this book will delight and give pleasure
With the finest ingredients mixed in good measure.
It will give food for thought and nourish the soul
Whether used as a dip or read as a whole.
It is salted with wit and peppered with grace
Sauced with good humour and more than a trace
Of wisdom and learning are found in each page
To delight every reader, whatever their age.
It is a gracious companion and an excellent read
Its profits all going to those in most need.

PREFACE

In 1979 St Stephen Walbrook, the Carmen's guild church since 1934, closed for repairs and the Carmen's Company moved to another Wren masterpiece, St Michael Paternoster Royal, headquarters of the then Missions to Seamen. General Secretary Bill Down was appointed Chaplain, and joined the Livery.

Faced with the formality of the Livery function, he combined his duty, Christian message and inimitable sense of humour in a rhyming grace, an innovation which became a welcome habit and eventually, a tradition maintained by his successors. Grace moved from custom and lip-service to anticipation and joy, bringing to the Carmen's table the needs of others and an appreciation of the privileges of fellowship.

In 1983 Bill became Chaplain to the Innholders and to the Farriers and extended this extra benison to their gatherings too, as he did for the Missions. Inevitably, his episcopal mission to Bermuda saw the words flow ever more rhythmically, and they continued on his return to English duties.

Some years ago it was suggested that he bring together the best of these in book form, to raise charitable funds for the Mission to Seafarers and Carmen's benevolence. As the collection grew, ideas for illustration emerged, and a lady Carman generously offered to provide them.

As the book took shape, we wanted to widen its scope, so that Bill's ministry could be better reflected, and he agreed to provide prayers and extracts from relevant sermons and his leaders in the Mission's *Flying Angel News*.

For a quarter century Bill Down has served the Carmen with dedication, wit and wisdom. We believe this book will raise a smile and lift the spirits with due reverence, ensuring his words reverberate beyond their original purpose to those who cannot help themselves.

Jeremy Gotch
Clive Birch

INTRODUCTION

When I was appointed Honorary Chaplain to the Worshipful Company of Carmen of London in 1979, one of my tasks was to say Grace before Company lunches, dinners and banquets. It was not long before I realised that Grace seemed to be a formality to be endured, rather than a relevant prayer for the occasion.

I decided to experiment, using rhyming verse, references to people, and incorporating an element of humour without irreverence. I am sure that the Almighty has a rich sense of humour, and I was encouraged when the response to Grace became positive and spontaneous.

A fellow Liveryman and Past Master of the Carmen's Company, Jeremy Gotch, persuaded me that a little book containing some of the Graces I had written would be welcome. It might also raise some funds for the Company and for the Mission to Seafarers, with whom I served happily for 27 years before my appointment as Bishop of Bermuda.

When I began to put the book together, another good friend, fellow Liveryman and Past Master, Clive Birch, became involved. He made many valuable suggestions and applied his comprehensive knowledge of publishing and printing to the project with great effect.

Another Past Master of the Company, John Ratcliff, became interested, and his wife Marsha Rae, a very talented artist and fellow Liveryman, graciously agreed to illustrate the book. She has done a magnificent job, and I am most grateful to her for her willing assistance.

An unexpected but pleasant surprise was the number of occasions when friends responded to Grace, and a selection of these responses is included in the collection.

In addition, at the request of fellow Liverymen, some prayers, sermon extracts, other verses and passages from leaders in the *Flying Angel News* have also been included.

The writing of Graces has given me enormous pleasure, and it has been very satisfying to realise that people were genuinely listening to what was being prayed for and were hopefully joining in themselves in spirit.

Bill of Fare

At a City Dinner, renowned for the length of the speeches

Bless us Lord
At this board
You afford.

Strike a chord
Lest we're bored
When we're jawed!

      Amen

An adaptation of a traditional Grace for a friend about to enter hospital, and for whom hospital food was not something to which to look forward

Give me a good digestion, Lord,
And something to digest.

Whence and how that something comes
I leave to Thee, who knowest best.

And as I face this hospital food
Keep me in a pleasant mood!

      Amen

Innholders

I was appointed Chaplain to The Worshipful Company of Innholders, following the death in 1983 of Prebendary Tom Kerfoot, who had served in that capacity for a significant number of years.

The Innholders have a magnificent Hall in the City on the opposite side of College Street from St Michael Paternoster Royal, the church and central office of the Mission to Seafarers.

I felt a particular affinity with the Innholders: I had been the licensee of the bar in the Flying Angel Club in Fremantle, Western Australia, in my previous appointment with the Mission!

At an Innholders' Company Dinner on 21 March 1989

We thank You, Lord, for our City fair,
We thank You too for all Your care.
We ask that You will grant our prayer
To bless our meal and this Company rare.

And bless, we pray, our good Lord Mayor.

    Amen

At an Innholders Dinner on 2 December 1986

We thank You, Lord, for food and drink,
And let us pray, as now we think,
That our meal tonight will make each bolder
To live his life a worthy Innholder.

    Amen

When I retired as the Honorary Chaplain of the Worshipful Company of Innholders, upon my appointment as Bishop of Bermuda, Judge Geoffrey Lovegrove, a Liveryman of the Company, wrote these verses

His Rhyming Grace

In their ancient Hall,
At the Beadle's call,
They mind the dreadful step,
Then stand in awe
Of the Canon's roar
As God's appointed Rep.

When Innholders meet
Back in College Street,
His Graces will be thought of . . . . . .
Their Shakespeare, Donne,
Pope, Blake, Anon,
Keats, Tennyson . . . . well, sort of.

May his Sermons be
In poetic Key,
With humour made the brighter.
The Word's no worse
In comic verse
From 'neath a Bishop's Mitre.

GREATNESS

What do you think makes a person great?

In commerce, greatness is sometimes equated with outstanding success. In politics, with an ability to speak compellingly. In art and music, with perfection of technique or flawless rendering of colour and sound, and in sport, with exceptional feats of prowess.

But are these adequate definitions? They may be the outward visible signs of greatness, but they are not to be mistaken for the essential inner and objective quality.

True greatness lies within a person, in what motivates them and develops their character and personality. It grows from an honest assessment of themselves, an acceptance of their humanity, a realisation that God loves them and is moulding them, and from having a vision of what might be achieved, and determination to succeed through utilising fully all the qualities and experiences God gives. It is how they use these talents that can turn ordinariness into greatness.

Jesus stressed the link between humility, service and greatness. '*You know that in the world rulers lord it over their subjects,*' He said. '*But it shall not be so with you. Among you, whoever wants to be great must be your servant.*' [Matthew 20 verses 25–28]

Extracts from my sermon at the Installation Service of the Master of The Worshipful Company of Innholders, 2 October 1984

Farriers

In 1983 when my highly respected and much loved predecessor as General Secretary of the Missions to Seamen, Prebendary Tom Kerfoot, died, he had also served as Chaplain to the Worshipful Company of Farriers, and I was honoured when the Company invited me to succeed him.

By then I was fully aware of the demands of the position, and I warned the Company of my likely occasional absences before accepting. For me it was a very happy and fulfilling appointment.

The Farriers' Prayer, which I was asked to write

O Lord God, we pray Thee to bless our Company
   of Farriers of this City.
Forge our characters on the anvil of Thy love.
Fit us to fulfil our vocation with skill, gentleness and
   patience.
Shoe us with the Gospel of Thy peace.
And give us grace, we pray, to serve Thee in our
   service of others;
Through Jesus Christ our Lord.

     Amen

At a Court dinner on 24 June 1985

Bless, O Lord, our Court of Farriers.
With food and drink we pray You'll marry us.

Bless the Master, here to guide us.
Bless the speakers, ne'er to chide us.

Bless the Clerk, here to harry us.
And bless the horses, home to carry us.

    Amen

At a Farriers' luncheon on 14 March 1986

Lord, bless this food
Splen-difer-ous.
May it put
No weight on us!

    Amen

At a Court dinner on 23 June 1989

Thank You, Lord, for food and wine,
And bless us as we sit to dine.

Bless the work of all the Farriers –
Between us may there be no barriers.

Prosper the aims for which we've fought,
And bless the members of the Court.

      Amen

At a dinner on 26 September 1986

Lord of all our times and dates,
Master of our dreams and fates,
Bless what comes upon our plates –
And bless our Master, Michael Mates.

    Amen

At a luncheon at the Savoy towards the end of John Alford's enjoyable and productive year of office as Master of the Company 27 July 1989

Thank You, Lord, for this fruitful year
Of work and plans and great good cheer.
Bless this meal, fruit of much toil.
Bless, we pray, the Princess Royal.
And with his year now almost gone,
Thank You for our Master John.

    Amen

At my final Company dinner, on 2 February 1990, before taking up my appointment as Bishop of Bermuda

For bread and meat and wine and beer,
For friends and guests all gathered here,
  We give You thanks, O Lord.

For all who food or shelter lack,
The stranger, poor, or bent of back,
  We pray to You, O Lord.

On this Company of Farriers –
At the bar renowned long tarriers! –
  Pour Your blessing, Lord.

Grant this request of the parting cleric –
  Bless, we pray, our Master Derek.

        Amen

The ROLE of a LIVERY CHAPLAIN

Throughout our lives we make new beginnings. Fresh openings, opportunities, crises and experiences confront us constantly, whether we like it or not.

The same principle applies to a Livery Company; changes occur regularly. New members are admitted; every year the Company has a new Master and Wardens; and occasionally there is a new Chaplain.

The Chaplain's role is seldom strictly specified, so let me spell it out.

He is not there just to say Grace before meals, nor just to dedicate gifts to the Company, nor because the Company has always had a Chaplain.

He is there to know those whom he is appointed to serve, to be their friend and confidant, and to be a priest among them.

The Bishop outlines a priest's calling at ordination. He is to be 'a servant and shepherd, to proclaim the word of the Lord, to lead his people in prayer and worship, to serve them with joy, and to search for his children in the wilderness of this world's temptations, and guide them through its confusions . . . .'.

The Good Shepherd, Jesus Christ, is the example for the priest, who is to care for those committed to his charge.

Extract from my first sermon as Chaplain of the Worshipful Company of Farriers, 13 September 1983

Carmen

I was invited to become Chaplain to the Worshipful Company of Carmen, a long-established Livery Company of the City of London, in 1979 and because, as General Secretary of the Missions to Seamen, I was travelling frequently to many parts of the world I thought long and hard before accepting.

I am very glad indeed that I did.

I discovered that this venerable Company still has an important role to play in the transport industry. I met many wonderful people in the Company, and made lifelong friends. As I came to know more and more members I found that I had a real and satisfying ministry among them; for some I was perhaps their only link with the Church. I enjoyed the formal occasions, and did my best to get them off to a lively start with a thought-provoking Grace before the meal.

The Carmen's Prayer, which I was invited to compose for the Company

O Lord our God, we pray Thee to bless our Company of Carmen of this City. May we be Thine for ever. May we fulfill our calling, both in providing the essential service of transport, and also in our good works. Grant that we may manifest Thy glory in the world, and finally come to Thine eternal Kingdom: through Jesus Christ our Lord.

Amen

At a Company dinner at which officers of the Royal Corps of Transport were honoured guests

Thank You, Lord, for food and wine,
Friends to greet, and hall to dine.
Thank You for this Royal Corps –
Transport experts to the core.
Bless our Company as we feed.
Succour all who are in need.
Thank You for too for each achiever,
Especially Master Christopher Leaver.

   Amen

The Company's formal Grace

Bless, O Lord, we pray,
  our Queen,
  our country,
  our Lord Mayor,
  our City of London, and
  our Company of Carmen.
Strengthen our bodies with this food and wine, for
  which we give you thanks.
Gladden our hearts with our fellowship.
Inspire us with love for one another and for You,
And make us mindful of the needs of others;
For Jesus Christ's sake.

     Amen

ACHIEVING AIMS

People employ various means to achieve their aims.

Some employ force. Some try to buy power. Some adopt intimidation. Some resort to dishonesty. Some use the force of their personality to obtain their ends.

Others, however, set out to achieve their purposes by firm adherence to high principles, strong self-discipline and a profound respect for others. They reflect the attitude commended by the prophet Zechariah: *'Not by might, nor by power, but by my Sprit, says the Lord of hosts.'*

This was how the Worshipful Company of Carmen conducted its affairs during the past year: with honour, firmness, discipline, gentleness, and respect for the individual members. Some of the words of Jesus established the tone: *'I am among you as one who serves; whoever wants to be great must be your servant.'*

The incoming Master's theme for his year in office is the challenge and struggle all of us face in life, and the mental, moral and spiritual armour we need to cope with this.

The armour God bids us wear is truth, integrity, commitment to peace, faith, and the power of His Word.

Extracts from my sermon at the Installation of Tony Hart as Master of the Worshipful Company of Carmen, 14 October 1982

At the lunch following the Installation of Her Royal
Highness the Princess Anne as Master of the Company on
23 October 1986

Lord of horsebox, coach and van,
Author of the master plan,
Bless our food, from oven or pan,
Bless our drink, from bottle or can,
Bless our Livery every man,
And bless our Master, Princess Anne.

    Amen

At a banquet in the Mansion House on 10 March 1987

Lord of sea and land and air,
Bless, we pray, our City fair.
Bless as well our good Lord Mayor.
Bless our guests, each woman and man;
Bless our feast (the Clerk's fine plan);
And bless our Master, Princess Anne.

    Amen

At a dinner on the occasion of the presentation of the
Company's Awards for professional and technical excellence
in 1986

Thank you Lord, for a place to dine,
Thank you too for food and wine.
Bless our guests, our friends, our meal –
Conviviality may we feel.
Bless the winners of each award;
Prestige and orders be their reward.
Bless our speakers, grant them levity,
Wisdom, wit, and above all – brevity!

    Amen

At a Court luncheon on 9 July 1997

Thank You, Lord, for this fine lunch –
The meat we chew, the bread we crunch,
The wine which packs a mighty punch.

Assist, we pray, all those in need,
Of every colour, race and creed,
And grant we help by word and deed.

May we never friendships botch;
Deliver us from too much Scotch!
And bless our Master, Jeremy Gotch.

    Amen

At a luncheon on 30 January 1990 when the Chaplain
relinquished office on appointment as Bishop of Bermuda

For bread and meat and wine and beer,
For friends and guests all gathered here,
  We give You thanks, O Lord.

For all who food or shelter lack –
The stranger, poor, or bent of back –
  We pray to You, O Lord.

On this our Company of Carmen –
Once the scourge of all the barmen –
  We ask Your blessing, Lord.

     Amen

The Worshipful Company of CARMEN'S CARNIVAL BALL

RAE

Gracious Companions

On being asked to say a prayer at the opening of a public house in London in 1988

O Lord God, whose Son Jesus Christ was born in the stable of an inn at Nazareth; who enjoyed the company of His fellow human beings; and who was a welcome guest at a wedding in Cana of Galilee; grant that this inn may be a place of welcome, fellowship and good cheer for all who enter. Bless all who serve here, and in serving others may they truly and faithfully serve You.

Amen

An adaptation of a well known anonymous Grace

God of goodness, bless our food.
Keep us in a pleasant mood.
Bless the cooks, and those who serve us –
And from indigestion, Lord, preserve us.
And if long speeches we endure,
Give us first a good liqueur!

     Amen

A general purpose Grace

For health and strength and life and love,
For all good gifts come from above.
We give you thanks, O Lord.

Bless this meal and us today,
All we do and all we say,
And for all in need, we pray.

     Amen

Missions to Seamen

Two thirds of my ministry ($26\frac{1}{2}$ years) were spent in the service and fellowship of the Missions to Seamen, the Anglican Church's outreach to the seafarers of the world, now re-named the Mission to Seafarers.

They were wonderful years.

For more than 11 years I served as port chaplain in South Shields, Hull and Fremantle in Western Australia. I visited more than 10,000 ships, and was in charge of important seafarers' centres. For more than 14 years I was the Society's General Secretary, and visited all its 118 centres at regular intervals. I found real fulfilment in my ministry among seafarers.

It was later in my time with the Society that I started to compose Graces, and I regret that the number in this section is not greater.

The IMPORTANCE of PRAYER

Every Christian knows that prayer is important – but no Christian I have known has ever been really satisfied with his or her prayer life.

I can see how my atitude to prayer has changed over the years.

As a child I prayed for many things – for success at sports and exams, for avoidance of trouble, for things I wanted and for speedy recovery when ill.

When I was 17 and seriously ill, it finally dawned on me that I was not the centre of the universe, and that there is a God in overall charge of everything and everyone. When I was 20 I heard a wonderful sermon, a turning point in my life, and I committed myself to love and serve Him.

I began to understand, to pray in earnest and yet, now more than 30 years later, I am far from satisfied with the quality of my prayer life.

Let's think about prayer from first principles. What is prayer? Prayer is speech addressed to God by people. It is how He makes known to us His will in ways we can understand. It is how we express our living relationship with Him.

Why should we pray? Because this is how God has chosen that we should communicate with Him. Because it is our lifeline to God.

How should we pray? We should pray as God in Jesus Christ taught us to pray – first for His will to be done on earth, His name to be respected and his Kingdom to come, and second for our daily needs.

Where should we pray? Wherever we happen to be – God is with us everywhere. We should pray regularly in Church with others and in a quiet place alone.

When should we pray? Regularly. Not once a year, once a month or once a week, but daily.

Who should pray? All of us need to pray. God needs us to pray.

For the committed Christian, prayer is not an optional extra. It is his lifeline to God.

Flying Angel News – December 1987

48

At a dinner in aid of the Missions to Seamen in the Painted
Hall at Greenwich on 28 April 1989

We give You thanks, O Lord of all,
For the beauty of this Hall.

We give You thanks for food and wine,
And for the friends with whom we dine.

Guide we pray this our Mission;
Bring its labours to fruition.

And giving thanks for all her toil,
Bless our President, the Princess Royal.

     Amen

ATTRACTIVE CHRISTIAN LIVING

The Gospel is communicated by quality of life. A dedicated Christian life is a most effective instrument of evangelism. Basic moral integrity, a disciplined lifestyle, a healthy outlook on life underpinned by a deep but simple faith, and a respect for others which does not seek to force personal convictions on them, all combine to make a powerful witness to the love and care of Christ and His Church. A committed Christian is soon recognised for what he or she is. In the seafaring community, and in particular on a ship, a Christian seafarer lives his faith under the daily scrutiny of people who see his every action and hear his every word, on duty and off duty. It is a real challenge to be a Christian on a ship.

From an address given to the International Christian Maritime Association Conference in New York in 1978

A lively dynamic voluntary helper at the Flying Angel Club
of the Missions to Seamen in Fremantle, Western Australia,
was celebrating her 40th birthday. I sent her this fax
message.

There was a young lady called Jill,
Who worked at the Club with a will.
  Now she's hit forty
  She'll never be naughty –
With love and best wishes from Bill.

A Gala Ball in aid of the Missions to Seamen was held at the
Baltic Exchange in the presence of Her Royal Highness the
Princess Royal, our President. The formal part of the
evening began with Grace before dinner: 31 October 1985

Lord of all,
At this ball
In this Hall,
May we all
At Your call
Have a ball!

    Amen

Grace at a Farewell Luncheon at the Royal Thames Yacht Club on 15 January 1990, organised by the Missions to Seamen and attended by its President Her Royal Highness the Princess Royal, prior to my taking my leave of the Society and setting out for Bermuda.

Thank You, Lord, for rum and gin,
Vintage wines from exotic bin,
Lovely food from oven and tin –
Ingratitude would be a sin.
Bless us all here gathered in –
And bless the new boss, Canon Glyn.

    Amen

At a dinner attended by graduates of Oxford and Cambridge Universities on Boat Race Night, 1 April 1995

Thank You, Lord, for Boat Race Night,
A time for fun and true delight
And memories of a well fought fight . . . .

Bless our banquet, fish or lamb,
Bread, and meat, and wine, and dram;
And bless us all, from Isis or Cam.

    Amen

Grace at a dinner of the International Maritime Industries
Forum on 27 March 1984

O Lord, guide and protect the world in which we
    live.
Grant peace between the nations.
Prosper our efforts in shipping and business.
Relive the needs of the poor and homeless.
Bless the food and drink we shall enjoy.
Grant that good fellowship and co-operation
    between us may flourish and increase.

And may all the speakers at this Forum
Instruct and enlighten, but never bore 'em.

    Amen

Grace at a leaving function on my last day of service with
the Missions to Seamen (the Flying Angel as it is known
because of its emblem) on 31 January 1990.

Bless The Mission is my song,
Keep the Angel flying strong.
Bless the new boss, Canon Glyn –
May he serve it without sin.
To stop this Grace becoming ruder,
Ship the Bishop to Bermuda!

    Amen

At a dinner in honour of the retiring Director of the
Maritime Society, Dr Ronald Hope, at Trinity House,
London, on 25 June 1986

For hope – in a world full of fear and gloom;
For hope – in the life of the world to come;
For hope – in the exciting work of the Marine
　　Society;
For hope – of a good dinner with good company in
　　a good place;
　　and
For Ronald Hope – leader, writer, educationalist,
　　colleague, and friend –
We give You hearty thanks, O Lord.

　　　Amen

SALT – what it can teach us

In His Sermon on the Mount, Jesus told His followers that they were 'the salt of the earth'.

I was once in Western Australia for the opening of the new Dampier Seafarers' Centre, 20° south of the equator, 900 miles north of Perth on the north-west shoulder of Australia, and an extremely hot place. After the opening I made a visit to Dampier Salt, a company which exports about 2 million tons of salt each year. The basic process is a simple one.

In a series of some 30 large rectangular ponds, artificially constructed on flat, low land right by the sea, sea water is pumped in and allowed to evaporate, thus eventually leaving a thick layer of salt to be harvested.

My thoughts then turned to the uses which are made of salt.

The human body needs a certain amount of salt, and in hot countries many people take salt tablets to prevent dehydration.

Salt is widely used in the preparation of food for adding flavour.

It is widely used in the preservation of food; in the days before refrigeration, salt meat and salted provisions formed a large part of the seaman's diet.

It also has antiseptic and cleansing qualities. As a boy I can remember gargling with salt and water if I had a sore throat.

Salt flavours, preserves and cleanses, and its pure white colour sparkles in the light.

Jesus told his followers that they were 'the salt of the earth', which was a description both of their present role and also of their calling:

They were to be a wholesome influence or flavour in the world; they were to be preservers of high standards in business and family life and in all their actions, and they were to be a cleansing influence in a world where evil is all too apparent.

Those words of Jesus to His earliest followers apply equally to His followers in every age. As His followers, we are, and we are called to be, 'the salt of the earth'.

Do our lives reflect this?

Extract from my General Secretary's column in Flying Angel News – October 1980

Bermuda

On 25 January 1990 I was consecrated as Bishop of Bermuda, where we spent almost six years. There were many occasions, both formal and informal, when I was invited to say Grace before meals. In the selection which follows I have included several responses by others.

The following verse, written by a member of the choir of the Bermuda Cathedral, appeared in the *Diocesan News* soon after my arrival in Bermuda as Bishop

Bishop Bill

Our Bishop is a jolly man,
Now just what we did need.
He's only small, yet ten feet tall
To guide his flock indeed.
He likes a joke, does not provoke,
And smiles a lot, I'll say;
But when it comes to serious stuff
He's there to lead the way.
It's nice to have a jolly man,
He makes you laugh at times;
It shows he's only one of us,
And just the humble kind.
So let us pray for him each day,
And hope he'll stay a while.
Our Bishop Bill, a jolly man –
We really like his style.

Hilde Leary

The Registrar of the Diocese of Bermuda was a delightful, distinguished and highly efficient solicitor, Michael Woods. He was also a good friend, and my golfing partner. As a token of my appreciation of his services I presented him with a box of his preferred yellow golf balls, accompanied by this limerick 9 April 1994.

There once was a lawyer named Woods,
Who rejoiced in his wife's tasty puds.
  His great contribution
  To a legal solution
Was to always deliver the goods!

to which Michael replied with the lines overleaf

The Registrar was very pleased
When his best client gently eased
A dozen golden golf balls in
To his capacious lawyer's fin.
Said he "The Bishop's bounty will
Be struck beyond the highest hill
And spread around the countryside
To left and right, ahead, beside;
I shouldn't even really mind
If one or two end up behind.
I'll hit 'em over every brook
No matter if I slice or hook,
Or yet contrive to miss or top 'em
With any luck I'll really whop 'em".
Tony and Alistair will stand
And marvel at the careless hand
Which treats a dozen brand new missiles
With less respect than the Epistles,
Which this poor golfer closely studies
Before he rushes out and muddies
The sparkling sea round Riddell's Bay
With fall-out from his fierce essay
To win the morning's friendly foursome
With shots that strike his friends as awesome.
In brief, this gift gave me great pleasure
And will enhance our mutual leisure.

At a luncheon hosted by the ladies of Bermuda Cathedral for a visiting group of Church people from Manchester, Connecticut, in the USA

Thank You, Lord, for Christian friends
Who visit us from earth's wide ends.
Thank You too for food and talk,
Chicken, beef and good roast pork.
Give help we pray to all in need
Through loving thought and word and deed.
Bless us all this happy day,
Especially our friends from the USA!

    Amen

When British Airways in Bermuda were renewing their office furnishings and equipment, a rather fine office/desk chair was surplus to requirements. When it was offered to me, I accepted it with alacrity. I always felt kindly disposed to the Chairman of BA (Lord King) thereafter! 10 August 1992

The Bishop has got a new chair
From friends in good British Air.
  As the telephones ring
  He feels like Lord King –
But he doesn't yet have the white hair!

On the 1995 installation of a fax machine in the office of a friend in Bermuda I sent him the following fax

Praise God from whom all Faxes flow.
Praise Him all creatures here below.
Praise Him above, ye heavenly host –
The Fax is better than the post!

DEAR BISHOP
BILL DOWNS
A FAX TO
LET YOU KNOW
YOUR DESK
CHAIR IS
ARRIVING
BEST REGARDS
LORD YONG

A Trafalgar Night Grace at a dinner of the Royal Navy
Officers' Association held in the Royal Bermuda Yacht Club
on 21 October 1991

For food, and wine, and company fine;
For a handsome room in which to dine;
  We give You thanks, O Lord.

For Nelson's courage, and Nelson's deeds;
For Trafalgar's glory, and meeting needs;
  We give You thanks, O Lord.

        Amen

At Harvest Supper for the Bermuda Cathedral Choir on 16 October 1992, under the able guidance of the Organist and Choir Mistress, Ruth Henderson

Thank You, Lord, for Harvest fare,
Prepared for us with loving care......
Thank You for our marvellous choir –
May their notes rise higher and higher!
A special thanks for Mistress Ruth,
Whose teaching always rings with truth.
Bless the food on every plate,
And guide us if we get home late!

     Amen

Our daughter Helen decided to portray in Chaucerian style a cameo of our life in Bermuda. She was amused by the names I had given to the fish in the small pond in the garden of Bishop's Lodge, and by my response at the scene when Sally fell in the street and slightly hurt herself

A Bishoppe ther was, a jolly manne,
Who with chaplains liked to sip a canne.
At sermones al otheres he did excel:
In twelve minutes he could alweys tel
A tale nautical, or eek relate
How frightening and fearful is the state
Of one who's being mobbed. A pond he hadde
Wherein did dwell many fishes madde:
Saddam Hussein, John Major, George Bushe.
He loved to feed them – but alas, one pushe
Would dampen episcopal attire
And cause floating fisshes to expire.
He pulls no rank, gentle as a lamb,
Quoth he: "I simply tell them who I am."
A WYF he hadde, a verray batte winge,
Who loathed floures, and this chose to singe.
One morn while hasting ducklike hir weye,
Hir bunioned foote did sadly streye.
Down ful on hir comely face she felle.
Hir housbonde, passing, seyde "Oh, to helle
With all thise wrecched dronk women folk!"
But he did stoppe, being a godly bloke
And lo! did act the Good Samaritan.
In his arms scooped up the hapless Gran.
Although she queasy felte, and somdeel ill,
Still uttered those oft used wordes, "Oh Bill!"

Helen Burn (née Down)

At a dinner at The Cottage (the official residence of the Senior Royal Naval Officer in Bermuda) on the closure of HMS *Malabar*, the Royal Navy base, and the retirement of Commander Robin Bawtree RN, as Senior Naval Officer, Bermuda, in 1995

Thank You, Lord, for food and wine,
The splendour of this house to dine,
  And specially for this company fine.

Thank You for the Royal Navy –
Regular, Reserve, and Wavy –
  Protecting us from grim old Davy.

We pray for all in want or need,
Of every country, race and creed;
  May we help by word and deed.

Lord, bless our food, roast or flan,
Bless our drinks, from bottle or can;
  And bless the Bawtrees, Robin and Anne.

     Amen

At a dinner in May 1994 to celebrate the 50th anniversary of the granting of Women's Suffrage in Bermuda. The guest of honour was Baroness Blatch, Minister of State at the Home Office

Thank You, Lord, for women of vision,
Courage, strength, and a sense of mission,
  Bringing good things to fruition.

Guide Bermuda, this isle without match –
A gleaming jewel in a watery patch –
  And bless our speaker, Baroness Blatch.

     Amen

At the end of their visit to Bermuda the Bishop of Montreal the Rt Rev Andrew Hutchinson penned the following verses on behalf of the visiting Canadian Bishops

When Bill asked the Bishops to come,
Church Society was almost struck dumb.
While the scheme was courageous
The cost was outrageous,
But Bill kept on beating the drum.
He appealed to Ted's piety,
And soon the Society
The depths of its pockets would plumb.
So we're here for a week
To take just a peek.
The island is beautiful,
And Bill's subjects most dutiful
In showing us all round the place –
The Governor, Premier, and even the clergy
All reverently bow for His Grace.
It's all been so splendid
We're sorry it's ended,
But ever so glad that we came.
One wonders, however,
If Bermuda will ever
Again after this be the same.
So thanks to you both, Bill and Sally,
By our troth it's the unanimous tally,
 That this is the best –
 Forget all the rest! –
Meeting we've had of the House.

You've won our affection
With every confection,
Which goes for each Bishop and spouse.

Dinner at Government House in Bermuda on 20 October 1992 celebrating the arrival of the new Governor of Bermuda, Lord (David) Waddington

For this House, so fair and tall,
Where Governors welcome one and all –
  We praise Your name, O Lord.

For colleagues, friends, food and wine,
And for this kindly call to dine –
  We give You thanks, O Lord.

For ourselves, keep us free from greed,
Assisting those who are in need –
  We pray to You, O Lord.

On these leaders of our land,
And David now our Governor grand –
  We ask Your blessing, Lord.

    Amen

At my sixtieth birthday party, the Registrar of the Diocese
of Bermuda, Michael Woods (who was also my golf partner),
produced this marvellous Chaucerian poem

The Bishop
There also was a Bishop of that place
Who tirelessly served and preached God's grace;
He visited his churches at swift pace
And always with a kind and cheerful word.

He stood upon no state as he progressed
But walked the streets like any honest friar,
Answering all, even if they were shrill,
And patiently and lovingly he heard

The prayers and hopes of people and of choir,
And always content to let them call him Bill.
He loved the oceans beautiful and wide
With special fervour throughout his whole life;

The mariners who sail the seven seas
Would be for him a fitting diocese.
And tender was he still to his dear wife
(At Cambridge both were learned in the arts
And there it was they stole each other's hearts),
And children four who lived in other lands.

He liked to hold a golf club in his hands,
And, swinging it with fearsome strength and speed,
While putting dextrously upon the greens,
Competed hard throughout all nineteen holes,
His pleasure at success a pretty scene

Enjoyed by those who joined him at that place
Where golfers congregate and dream their dreams,
Which, written down, but disappoint it seems.
As so he led his flock throughout the Isles
With vision and with purpose, and with smiles.

In truth he was a very proper prelate,
No honest folk would hesitate to tell it;
So when at length he reached his sixtieth year
A feast was set for all to wish him cheer.

WOMEN'S WORTH

When Jesus was born, women generally were held in low esteem. He gave them their proper dignity and value.

He re-affirmed Old Testament teaching. God created human beings male and female. He brings them together in marriage to be faithful companions for each other; to complement each other physically, mentally and spiritually; to reproduce; and to reflect God's love for us all.

During His earthly ministry Jesus welcomed the women of all backgrounds who came to Him. He recognised the shame, penitence and love of a prostitute, and made her feel accepted. He showed Mary of Magdala the vision and reality of a new way of life, and it was to her first that He appeared after His resurrection.

Since His death and resurrection the Living Jesus has made Himself known to millions of women and men. Some of these women have made a huge impact on the Church and the world. Joan of Arc inspired a whole nation. Mother Teresa won the attention and the goodwill of the whole world through her ministry to the poor and the dying in Calcutta.

The Church has been slow to recognise that its failure to afford women their due dignity and value has been both wrong and counter-productive.

Extract from my sermon in Bermuda Cathedral on 19 December 1993

On attaining my sixtieth birthday a splendid party was held at Bishop's Lodge, Bermuda. My wife Sally wrote the Grace on 15 July 1994

Lord, thank You for this festive fare,
And all these friends who've come to share.
Relieve, we pray, the poor and needy;
Protect them from the mean and greedy.
Bless all our guests, both dames and blokes;
Be with us in our chats and jokes.
And bless, O Lord, our Bishop Bill,
With joy tonight his cup full fill.
Give him support in times of woe,
And strength to face the big Six-Oh!!

  Amen

Family and Friends

In December 1988 Sally's much-loved father died, and her mother came to stay with us over Easter in 1989. This was our Grace at lunch on Easter Sunday

Thank You, God, for Easter joy –
Nothing can its peace destroy.
Thank You for our Risen Lord,
And for His presence at our board.
Thank You, God, for Easter cheer;
And thank You too that Grandma's here.

     Amen

81

A limerick composed on 20 July 1988 at a dinner in Guildhall in the presence of HRH the Princess Royal: the Chaplain was seated next to the Lady-in-Waiting, and the Princess Royal's Private Secretary, Colonel Peter Gibbs, was sitting at the foot of the table. When the waitress serving the main course inadvertently poured all the gravy from the roast lamb over the Lady-in-Waiting's evening dress, and the Chaplain did his best to mop up, the Colonel loudly and amusingly rebuked the Chaplain for his clumsiness!

The Lady-in-Waiting, no less,
Had gravy poured over her dress.
  The Colonel said "Bill,
  Do much better still;
You've made one helluva mess!"

The Canon said "Peter, you twit!
I'm not such a terrible nit.
  The error was made
  By a nice serving maid,
Who did it, and muttered 'Oh, ... bless me!' "

My father introduced me to golf when I was eleven years old, and I took to it quickly. A long illness in my late teens prevented me from playing for several years, and opportunities to play later in life were restricted. I have never managed to achieve a low handicap, but I play the game well enough to enjoy it, and badly enough not to worry about it!

A grace written for friends enjoying a golfing holiday in Kent

Lord of heaven, earth and sky,
Master of fairway, green and lie,
Ruler of Sandwich, Deal and Rye,

Thank You for each splendid course,
For challenging holes, and clinging gorse;
For steady grip, and driving force.

Thank You for this meal together.
Thanks for golf, whatever the weather;
And keep us from reaching the end of our tether!

     Amen

Leicester

When family concerns led us to return to England from Bermuda at the end of 1995, we spent the last $5\frac{1}{2}$ years of my full-time ministry in Leicester, where I was Assistant Bishop of the diocese and Priest-in-Charge of St Mary's, Humberstone.

For one memorable year, 1998/1999, I combined the functions of Bishop Commissary (in temporary charge of the diocese), Lord Mayor's Chaplain, and Priest-in-Charge of my parish. Occasions when I was asked to say Grace were many and various, as the selection which follows indicates.

As we were preparing to leave Bermuda for Leicester, a fierce hurricane ravaged the islands. In our garden were several avocado trees, heavy with almost ripe fruit. The hurricane took them all.

In a fax to the Bishop of Leicester's Personal Assistant, Penny Russell, I wrote:

Oh where, oh where have my lovely pears gone?
Oh where, oh where can they be?
  They went with the wind,
So surely I sinned –
And somebody else has them now!

Christmas dinner for the officers of the Leicestershire
Constabulary on 18 December 1998

We thank You, Lord, for our Police,
Who jump on crime, stop quick decease,
Guard Christmas turkeys and our geese.

We thank You, too, for Christmas cheer –
Turkey, sausage, mince pies and beer;
Bless all, we pray, who're gathered here.

Uphold this Force. Give it self-belief.
Let every crime come soon to grief.
Bless, O Lord, good David our Chief.

     Amen

At a dinner marking the appointment of the Chief Constable of Leicestershire, Keith Povey, to a new position 25 April 1997

Thank You, Lord, for our Police,
Staunch defenders of the peace,
  Cracking down on those who fleece.

In car or train, on road or heath,
Into his job he sinks his teeth;
  Bless the Chief, our good friend Keith.

        Amen

As Chaplain to the Lord Mayor of Leicester one of my tasks was to say Grace at civic dinners. At one on 14 December 1998 Mr Justice Scott Baker was Guest of Honour

Thank You Lord for the blessings of the Law,
Upholding what's right, giving wrong no door,
And chastising every thieving paw.

For our meal we give thanks to our Maker.
May each guest be a hearty partaker.
And bless, we pray, Mr Justice Scott Baker.

        Amen

OBSERVING the MILLENNIUM

A lot of nonsense has been written and talked about the Millennium, as the following extract from a national newspaper illustrates:

'Have you noticed how desperate the Church of England is to get in on the Millennium act? How they want to stamp their name on every aspect of it on the grounds that it is Christ's party and they'll cry if they want to . . . .'

It went on to ridicule the distribution of Millennium candles. For sheer breath-taking crassness that takes some beating!

Think of what the Millennium is.

❖ It is the 2000th anniversary of the birth of Jesus Christ. It is a specifically Christian occasion.

❖ It is a time for Christians to celebrate what Jesus accomplished by His life and death and resurrection. He showed us God Himself in action.

❖ It is a time to celebrate what God has accomplished through His Church throughout its history. The Church has led the way in education, healthcare, art, music, law-making and responsible citizenship.

❖ It is a time for Christians to proclaim the Good News proudly, joyfully and without apology.

So what is this about 'the Church of England getting in on the Millennium act?'

Nonsense!

Extract from my article in News and Views, *the monthly newssheet of Leicester Diocese, June 1999*

At a luncheon hosted by the Chief Constable of
Leicestershire at the beginning of a Police and Church
Leaders consultation on 28 August 1998

Thank You, Lord, that we are here
To meet the Chief and share good cheer.

Guide we pray our consultation,
Taking place in this fine station.

May our words be clear and brief –
And bless, we pray, our friend the Chief!

     Amen

At a dinner hosted by the Chief Constable of Leicestershire,
David Wyrko, on St George's Day 1999 in honour of the
High Sheriff of Leicestershire, Mrs Alison Wilson, and the
Chairman of Leicestershire County Council, Mrs Cordelia
Brock

Thank You, Lord, for good St George,
Whose trusty sword, honed on the forge,
  Closed forever the dragon's gorge.

Bless our Guests, a happy flock –
Alison Wilson, truly a rock,
  And County Chairman, Delia Brock.

     Amen

At a dinner of the Leicestershire Law Society, whose
President was John Crane, on 9 February 2001

Thank You, Lord, for the gift of the Law –
For judges, solicitors, barristers who jaw.

Thank You for those involved in our Courts,
Upholding the right, protecting all sorts.

Thank You for friends and this company fine.
Thank You too for our food and our wine.

As we enjoy both grape and the grain,
Please bless the President good John Crane.

     Amen

At a dinner of the Britain Australia Society in Leicester on 18 October 2000, the speaker was the appropriately named Tom Fremantle

We want to thank You, Lord, because
We love the sunny land of Oz.

We thank You for their wine and beer –
We'll drink them all with gusto here.

Bless our meal, and all who're here –
May we all enjoy good cheer.

With pleasure watch the speaker's mantle
Alight upon good Tom Fremantle.

     Amen

In 1999 the *Leicester Mercury* – a respected daily publication
– celebrated its 125th anniversary. At a civic dinner to
celebrate the occasion the Guest of Honour was Editor
Nick Carter

Thank You, Lord, for the world of papers –
The *Mercury,* its editor, opinion-shapers –
  And the joys of watching all their capers! . . .

Bless our meal, right from the starter.
May indigestion find no martyr.
  And bless our friend, the good Nick Carter.

    Amen

When I retired, the Bishop of Leicester hosted a dinner of the senior staff to wish us well. His chaplain, the Reverend Graham Johnson, produced a wonderful Grace, reflecting my love of Cricket, 24 June 2001

Lord of Hutton, Lord of May,
Lord of Smith (that's M.J.K.),
Lord of Gatting, who lost his cool,
Lord of the Bishop of Liverpool;
Captain of the English band
Feed us with your Dexterous hand.

Lord of Laker and of Lillee,
Lord of Davidson and Dilley,
Lord of Snow and Valentine,
Lord of Larwood's Bodyline,
Lord of Qadir, the great leg spinner,
Bless this Bishop's Staff Ramadhinner.
Lord of Grace Road, Lord of Kent,
Lord of Bridge across the Trent,
Lord of rain-swept Old Trafford,
Lord of Hove and Lord of Lord's,
Bless this evening, may we eat our fill,
And Lord bless Sally and Lord bless Bill.

      Amen

After All

WEARING UNIFORM

Now that I am retired, I wear my clerical collar only when I am actually on Church business, and I have become accustomed to being anonymous in the street. It comes as quite a shock when, if I happen to be wearing clerical attire, strangers greet me. Thinking about this recently reminded me of an incident when I was travelling abroad.

In 1981, I was visiting North America as General Secretary of the then Missions to Seamen and I was in a departure lounge at Houston International Airport in Texas. There were five departure gates and, as it happened, aircraft were due to leave from all five gates within the space of half an hour. The lounge was crowded.

I was standing alone, my back resting against a wall. I was dressed in a dark suit and wearing a black shirt and clerical collar. My thoughts were miles away.

Suddenly a smartly dressed young woman approached me. 'Excuse me, Father,' she said. 'Will you give me a blessing?' I agreed willingly, and she bowed her head. As I blessed her, I was conscious of many pairs of eyes focusing on us. When I had finished, she thanked me graciously, and returned to her group.

A few minutes later she returned. 'Father,' she said, 'I'm scared of flying. It was great to see a priest here in uniform. I just wanted to be blessed before flying, and I'm much calmer now.' With a lovely smile, she went on her way.

I have often reflected on that moment. I was travelling on the Lord's business, so it was appropriate to be easily identifiable. The opportunity to be of service would not have arisen had I not been dressed as a priest. How important it is to be ready to witness to our faith at any moment in any place.

The Save The Children Fund held a dinner in a new and striking hall to thank and encourage their supporters in Wales. The Princess Royal was present in her capacity of President of the Fund. I was asked to supply an appropriate Grace.

For mountains, streams and glorious vales,
And Save The Children's work in Wales,
  We give You thanks, O Lord.

For food and friends and lovely wine
Served in this Hall of bold design,
  We give You thanks, O Lord.

Bless our meal and these friends so loyal,
In this good cause so keen to toil,
  And bless, we pray, the Princess Royal.

    Amen

A Grace for every golfer

Almighty God,
  Whose Royal and Ancient Will it is
  That we should thank You for Your bounty,
Bless we pray our meal.
May each course be in perfect condition –
  the fish well hooked,
  the meat well sliced,
  the greens firm and true,
  the water no hazard.
So may we fly high with albatrosses,
  be strong like eagles,
  and gentle as birdies;
And, with St Andrew, may we
Achieve par for the course of life.

    Amen

SAYING THANK YOU

I have often been moved by receiving letters from people thanking me for my ministry. One which gave me particular satisfaction came from an overseas seaman, whose name I was unable to decipher, in my early days as Port Chaplain at Hull. This is what he wrote.

'I'm the man you met in The Mission of the Fly Angel. Or is it The Blue Angel the name? I remember the Angel name, but I don't know if it was the name of the place or the name of the people that were there. I must say "thanks", but thanks very much for the moments we spent together, talking, dancing, or just only feeling some human near other one. It was the first time in my life that I have been in some place like this one. I never went before because I thought that always the people of this place would speak in every moment about religious worlds. But I found people with just only the feeling for to give friendship to the people that want and need it. If my English would be no more good, I would can tell some more things, but I just only know one word that can complete the idea that I have in myself, and that word is "thanks".'

He made all of us at the Flying Angel feel very much appreciated.

I recently visited a friend who was ill and having a rough time. When he was better, he wrote this verse, with its tongue-in-cheek twists, to make sure we don't feel too good about ourselves!

There's nothing so cheering when you are ill
  As getting a visit from dear Bishop Bill.
Though one asks if he's come as a friend,
  Or as a priest to one nearing the end.

  To be sure, I just hope it's the former,
For I'd hate to think I'm a near gorner.
  Whichever it is, I'm grateful indeed
For his visit to me was his day's good deed!

John Ellison

And finally,

A GRACE FOR THE READER

Thank You, Lord, for what's in store –
Food to savour, wine to pour.
Help the needy and the poor,
   and
Strengthen us to serve You more.

         Amen

THE CARMEN'S CHARITY

In common with all City Livery Companies, Carmen place great store on benevolence.

Their Benevolent Trust is autonomous, and its policy is simple – giving a little where it means a lot.

The priority is needy Carmen and individuals in need who have a transport or Carmen link.

The causes it supports are linked to the City and transport, education and health, with an emphasis on children, terminally ill and carers.

Its funds are not ancient or extensive, but built through the generosity of members, fund raising and careful investment.

In a world of need, Carmen care.

RAE

LIST of ILLUSTRATIONS

SUBSCRIBERS

Presentation copies

Her Royal Highness, the Princess Royal
The Worshipful Company of Carmen
The Mission to Seafarers
The Worshipful Company of Innholders
The Worshipful Company of Farriers
The Diocese of Bermuda
The Diocese of Leicester

Sally Down
MarshaRae Ratcliff
Jeremy Gotch KStJ
Clive Birch MBE
Sue Adams
A.J.D.Locke
E.Minugh
A.T.Imm
Eddie Black
Allan Highfield
Robin D. Waite
Colin Fleming & Licia Martin
Jennifer James
Col G.T.Spate OBE TD DL
Don Cleaver
Simon Cleaver
James Cowell
Charles W.Lloyd
Francis J.S.Ward
M.A.S. O'Donnell
L.M.Jones
Graham R.Westcott
Michael Taylor
Alan Millinder
Christopher Bullock
G.G.Fiegel
John C.F.Cameron
Prof Sir Robin Barbour
Michael Power
John Stacpoole
James Stacpoole

Bob Russett
Grace Russett
Richard Pye
Doug Ridley
B. L.Veale
Alistair Reason
Leslie Reason
Nigel Josling OBE
Peter Benson CBE
Nicholas Laister
Anthony Allen
Arthur White
Chris Knott
Kevin & Jacqui O'Shaughnessy
John G.Turner
Janet Gotch
Chris Gotch
Sarah Ford
Jenny Holmes
Alan Morgan
Bob Sturgess
I.P.Ramsay
John Wilmshurst
Mark Wynn
J.C.Harrison
Raymond C.Horsley
John Ellison
Major John H.Burgess
Edmund Farley
Alan Tilson
Nicky Dill

Commander Robin Bawtree OBE RN
His Worship the Mayor of Hamilton, Bermuda
W.J.C.Parlane
Kevin Fitzmaurice
Major Kevin Tuhey QVRM TD
Adrian Sellars
K.R.Thurtell
Col R.G.Cross
Richard Coles
R.Miller
Jean & Gerald Golder
Rev Alistair Helm
Margaret Terry
David Wyrko
Rev David White
Chris Eyre
Rev Martin Court
Dan Nicholas
John Stanton
David Glossop
Rev Miles Newton
Michael J.Gerson
Rev J.A.G.Scott
P. J.Crawshaw
F.W.H.Coles
The Rt Rev Tim Stevens
Miss M. Angus
Rev Anthony W.Wheeler
Rev F.L. Burnham
Mrs D.M.Connor
Ross Coad
Derek Redman MBE
Mrs E.A.Casebow
Rev Monty Ellson
Mrs S.P.Rogans
Phyllis O'Leary
Eric & Heather Britt
Mrs P.A.Lucas
Col J.C. Lucas OBE
Mrs Doreen M.Saunders
Mrs D.M.Barnicoat
T.Hughes
Ronnie King
Stephen Britt

John Ross
Geoffrey Simpson
C.C.B. Willis
K.R.Taylor
Miss M.S.Watts
Bernard Evan-Cook
Margaret Sherriff
M.A.Baugh
Mrs Jean Webster
J.C.Islip
John Ratcliff CBE
Ray Burrows
Arthur Kennedy OBE
W.G.Ogle
Margaret Hall
Roy Kirk
Olga Waterfield
Archbishop Bruce Stavert
Mrs Sylvia Price
Mrs M.T.M.Hayes
Margaret Zientek
Jan Edward Zientek
Mrs Peta Walmisley
Mrs June Mawdsley
Peter & Vivien Hardy
Veronica Palmer
Rev David Hanwell
Russell Graham Southern
Colin Mills
Telfer Saywell
Mrs E.A.Price
J.M.Davies
Rev Randolph V.N.Albano
Geoffrey & Gillian Carter
John & Joyce Theaker
Doreen Weston
David Brown
Nicholas Carr
Joan Garner (The Cash)
Mrs Pat Hodgson
Gerry A.Long

Remaining names unlisted